A Fostered Life

A Novel Based on True Student Journals

By Jean Rivot

Forward

In my years of being an English teacher in middle and high school, I had many students who were in foster care. When I assigned students to journal, they wrote what was on their minds, usually with nothing held back. Many wrote about their experiences in foster care. Some of them told me verbally what was happening to them because they either trusted me, or were at their bursting points and were desperate for help. Even though this story is fiction and the events happen to one young boy, it is a compilation of the journal entries and events that happened to my former students in real life.

Contents

Being Eleven

Being an eleven year old boy is tough. Sometimes I feel much older than I am. I know a lot, but grownups keep telling me that I don't know anything. Well, they're wrong. I'll bet they don't really remember how it feels to be a kid, or what we think, or why we think it. Kids know when it's time to run away. But there are forces we have no control over that keep us where we are. On top of that, my one refuge gets pulled out from under me. It was the only one I had, the only place to turn when things got really bad. My grandmother died. She was the only family I knew and the only one who truly seemed to care about me. I had no one else, except a completely absent father whom I haven't seen in six years. I don't even remember what he looks like. I only got to see my grandmother once a week, and she was the only person who ever hugged me. She was the only person who ever told me she loves me and the things only a grandmother would tell her grandchild. And now she's gone and I'm alone. I cried by myself because the people I was staying with didn't care. Did I tell her I loved her the last time I saw her? I couldn't remember. No one on this earth loves me anymore. I'm empty, lost in a sea of strangers.

What Do You Do With a Drunken Sailor?

The foster father in this house builds sailboats. Well, sort of. Tom is a drunk and mean and loud. He has a rough beard, because he shaves only once in a while and has a potbelly and skinny bowed legs. He spends most of his time pretending to work on his boats in his shop, which is a building off the long dirt driveway of the house. The shop is bigger than a garage and he keeps the refrigerator in there stocked with beer, which he begins to drink early in the day. By the time I get home from school, he's as mean as a wild boar. He yells at me just for walking from the sidewalk to the house. He calls me names, slurring them from lips he can't seem to control any longer. Some I've never heard before and some I can't understand. I try hard to stay away from him. I saw a movie once at someone's house called Dr. Jekyll and Mr. Hyde. That's what I nicknamed him in secret.

If You Want to Make God Laugh, Tell Him Your Plans

I closed my eyes to focus on what I had planned out for the past few weeks. I would steal the small boat Tom had just built and get away from here. I had gone over it a hundred times in my head. I knew what would be the perfect timing. It was going to be risky, but worth it if I could pull it off. I waited for midnight to arrive and when it did, I quietly sneaked out of my room then out of the house. Tom would be passed out from all his drinking and Kara snored so loud that I could hear her from my room. I could hear her now. I got to the workshop, and looked at my new freedom. It was small, but sleek and just waiting for me on a flatbed with tires, which made it easier to steal because the tires were quiet.

Stealing the boat didn't bother me. I had stolen a few things before, candy bars, a notebook, things like that. But I never stole anything this big before. I didn't care that it wasn't mine. I made it mine.

Slowly and quietly, I pulled it out of his shop and walked it down to the shore, only a half mile from here. This was not just any sailboat. This one was built like it was just for me, just for my size. It was ten feet long, and I knew it could carry me to any horizon I wished. I think Tom called it a sunfish. It seemed almost too easy to steal.

I watched people sail on the sound for weeks now. I saw what they did and how they did it and I knew I could do it, too. One day, this kid I met on the shore took me out on his boat and he even let me steer it. I felt a freedom I had never felt before. He was a nice kid, probably around fifteen, and when we got back to shore he told me I should ask my parents if I can go on an all-day sail with him. Fat chance of that happening.

When I got my boat on the water, I raised the sail and put my hands on the tiller and boom, just like the boy showed me. I didn't care that it was dark. I got used to the dark a long time ago. The wind was light, but enough for the sail, and the sea almost calm. My sailboat skimmed almost silently over the sheet of glass below, cutting through it like the sharpest of swords. It was my sword, my way out. I don't know how long I sailed for, but I found out that sailing at night made it hard to see land. I looked for lights, but they came in groups and I could not tell from this distance if they were houses or businesses. But I didn't want to head for lights. I wanted to head for a remote, empty place. But it was too hard to see.

There had to be someplace to sail to, I kept telling myself. When I did see the shore, it was so full of trees and darkness that I didn't want to get out there. Maybe I am afraid of the dark sometimes.

I had no choice but to turn back because I couldn't find open land to head toward, no matter how far I sailed. I must have sailed for hours when I finally found the place I began. I tied up the boat and could see the sky just begin to lighten before dawn, so I knew I had a good chance of getting back into the house without Kara and Tom waking up yet. I pulled the empty flatbed behind me and returned back to the place I never wanted to be. Back home, back to my foster parents, the third ones I have had this year alone.

I was at the first home this year for only a month. Michelle, the foster mother, got cancer and could not take care of me anymore. She was nice at first, but when she got sick and had to have surgery, she had no energy to do anything except lay in bed. I had to learn to make my own meals, wash my own clothes and clean, on top of school and homework. It didn't feel like a family. Sure, I felt bad for her because no one wants cancer, but I still felt deserted. Maybe that was selfish, but I couldn't help it. I needed someone, too. Someone who cared about me and could take care of me like every other kid out there has.

The second home I was taken away from because the foster dad had too many drunk driving arrests and the court decided it was an unfit home. I wasn't surprised about it because he was drunk a lot. When I saw how he acted, I decided I was never going to drink alcohol, even when I was old enough.

People thought I was shy because I didn't talk much. But it was because I never felt like I belonged. I had to constantly "feel out" people in order to sense their moods, or their reactions, or their behaviors. When you get switched around a lot from family to family, developing a sense for people quickly is important.

I learned that some people smile with their mouths, but not with their eyes. Those were the ones I had to be especially careful around. They usually hide their real feelings behind turned up corners of their lips. Eyes that don't smile are easy for kids like me to see. Some adults smile even when they are not happy to begin with. But other adults seem to miss that. My case workers were always too busy to notice. Well, maybe they did, but they didn't let me know, or maybe they had to pretend they didn't just to get their jobs done. I learned what eyes show pain, meanness, sadness, fear, drunkenness, even anger. It could mean survival for me to be able to do this, and soon it became second nature.

Now I was with people named Kara and Tom. I should feel lucky they even told me about my grandmother.

"Your grandmother died this morning. Caseworker called," Kara said when I walked through the living room. Her eyes didn't even look my way. Tom got up from his chair and went to the kitchen.

I felt my stomach and throat tighten, then a lot of pressure in my chest. They left me on the living room chair to cry by myself. They told me and just walked away.

At least I was able to cut school two days later and go to her funeral. I had known enough to look in the paper for her obituary, even though I had to sneak it into my room to find it. I didn't even consider that Tom or Kara would take me to her funeral because they would probably just laugh at me or something. I didn't matter to them.

Walking back to the shop, I waited to make sure the coast was clear, and I pulled the empty flatbed back, and left it there empty, for my foster father to wake up and wonder what had happened. He reported it stolen, but never suspected me for a minute. I never saw a man as angry as him when he discovered the empty flatbed. He started throwing things around in his workshop, stomping and swinging his arms, yelling,

"If I ever catch who did this, he's a dead man."

Lying Eyes

Two days later, I entered the church where my grandmother's funeral was being held. It was a little church, mostly white inside and the pews were a dark mahogany, which made them seem to jump out at you. I had only been in a church a few times, depending on the foster family I was staying with. Some of them went to church, but most of them didn't. When the ones that I went with would bring me, they would tell me if I didn't believe, I would go to hell. I guess they didn't know where I have lived.

There was a large stained glass window above the altar which added the only other colors in the church. My grandmother was laid out in the casket in front and there was a wreath of flowers on a stand next to her in the shape of a heart. I walked slowly to the front pew. I wasn't sure what to expect because I never went to a funeral before. I could hear myself breathing and my heart pounding in my chest. I didn't want to see her dead. I just wanted it to be a big lie. I looked around and saw about a dozen other people in there who I guessed were her friends.

I looked for a long time from the pew at my grandmother lying there. Her hair was pulled back, just like she always wore it, but she had makeup on that she never wore in real life. My throat felt tight and I couldn't swallow because I was trying not to cry. My heart was full of sadness that lost room to expand so it began to come out of my eyes. I wiped them quickly. Then I noticed something when I looked back at her. She was still breathing. Wait. Was she? Did they make a mistake? I looked at the other people. Did they notice that? No one seemed to see it but me. I looked back at her. I swore she was breathing. Am I crazy? I slowly walked up to the casket after a few other people did. When you're 11, people don't explain much about death and dying. I had to see for myself. I knelt down on the bar in front of the casket and stared at her face, then her chest. Was she breathing? I wasn't sure. I stood up. I took in a deep breath and ever so cautiously reached in and touched her arm. It was cold and hard. I grabbed my hand back and exhaled. I could sense the people in there following me with their eyes and shaking their heads. This could not be real.

I went sailing again as soon as I left there, this time in the light rain that lasted the rest of the day. The water was almost flat, even in the rain, just giving up small holes in it's surface where the raindrops hit. There was no view, with the exception of gray walls of the distant clouds and emptiness. I was alone out there, left on my own. As darkness began to arrive, and nowhere else to go, I had no choice but to once again, return to a family who didn't love me.

When I got home, Kara demanded to know where I was because the school had called. She called me a sneak and a liar. She said if I ever did that again, she would tell Tom and he would let me "have it", whatever that meant. She used that as a threat a lot. She sent me to my room and told me not to come out until the next morning for school. I was tired anyway. It was a long day.

How Dementia Affects the Young

My real father is in jail. One night he got more drunk than usual and he and my mother got into a bad fight. I was five at the time. He began to beat my mother badly. She couldn't defend herself and fell to the floor. Then he grabbed a kitchen knife, and, raging like a rabid wolf, stabbed her over and over right in front of me. He screamed and panted heavily when he finally stopped. That's when he noticed me. He picked me up, threw me in the back seat of the car, then went back in and threw her in the trunk. She was dead, or at least she looked like it. He threw something else in the trunk that I couldn't see. I was crying uncontrollably and my father kept yelling at me to shut up. I tried to, but couldn't, so I buried my face in my knees and arms. We drove to a dark, dirt covered wooded road, the only light being from the headlights. He finally stopped the car and told me to stay put when he got out. He took her out of the trunk and walked into the woods, dragging her dead weight behind him. He came back a few minutes later and took what I couldn't see before from the trunk: a shovel. I sat, scared out of my mind on this dark road and I couldn't stop crying. This couldn't be real. He came back to the car after I began to fear he was never going to come back. Then he drove back to our house and brought me inside, grabbed a beer from the refrigerator, turned on the TV, and sat in his easy chair, just like nothing had happened. Blood was everywhere, but it was like he didn't even notice. A little while later, my grandmother, his mother, walked into the house. She took one look around, asked where her daughter-in-law was, and got no answer. She picked me up, walked to a neighbor's house and called the police.

Like the way you pull a shade down in front of a window, or the way your hands cover your eyes at a scary part in a movie, I blocked this memory. I couldn't remember it at all, like when you ask an old person whose memory is gone what day it is. I had no idea my father was on death row. I knew my mother had died, but I was never told why. I'll find out someday where he is, though. And when I do, he and I will be together again. Forever.

Whenever I had asked my grandmother where he was, she would say he was working in another country and couldn't take me along. Something happened to my grandmother, too. She changed. Not in the sort of way that she didn't love me, but in the kind of way that she always seemed to be in a fog. She never wanted to do anything much anymore, and people came in to take care of her.

One day a lady with a policeman came to the door to take me away with them. I wasn't sure why and my grandmother had tears running down her face when we were leaving. I was crying and kept looking at her. She kept whispering, "I'm sorry, baby," as I was led away. They brought me to some place they called a "group home" where other kids were. I didn't know any of them, but they all looked scared, like me. I don't remember how long I was there for, it could have been two weeks or six months. I do remember that whenever someone new came to the home, when I turned to look at them, I always hoped it would be a familiar face. But it never was.

Musical Chairs

After that I was brought to a house and was told I was going to live there for awhile. I didn't know these people except that they had come to the group home once and tried to talk to me for a minute, but I didn't say anything. I just wanted my grandmother. My caseworker took me to her once a week in the nursing home they put her in. I was never so happy to see anyone in my life. I ran into her lap and arms and hugged her tight. She hugged me back, but it wasn't the strong hug I remembered. Most of that first visit with her, I just sat in her lap in her wheelchair and kept my arms around her neck and my head against her shoulder.

The family in the first foster house I lived in put me in a big bedroom with two bunk beds and three other kids who didn't look anything like each other. They were foster kids, too. Within three months, the parents got an unexpected job transfer to another state and couldn't take us with them. I didn't know foster kids with no blood relatives have to stay within their own state because no one ever told me that. Not that it mattered, because I didn't know anyone anywhere else, anyway. That was my first foster family. Now I was with my eleventh.

I usually got taken away from homes because of a lot of things. One time it was because I lived with a family who fought all the time. I don't mean just yelling, but hitting each other and screaming. I would escape to my room and bury my head in a pillow to try and block it out. I would cover my eyes, but it was hard not to hear what was going on, even when I would hug the pillow hard against my head and hum as loud as I could. Finally, during one of their fights, the foster mom had to go to the hospital from being hit so hard by her husband. The police had been called by a neighbor. That's when they stepped in and took all of us away from there. Even though I was never taught by anyone how to treat women, I knew I was never going to hit a girl. Where did they find these families who take kids in? When the school sent me to the psychologist after that, she kept asking me how that made me feel. I guess she thought it would make me remember what happened with my parents, but it never did. Those are secrets too deep for memories.

Sometimes I'd hear people say. "There's no place like home," but I didn't know why. There's plenty of places better than home.

The pounding on my bedroom door shook me awake from my nap. I jumped up as Kara, a woman with a hard looking face, stringy hair, cold, hard eyes, and a perfume of cigarettes, came in. She didn't say much, except, "Here," as she threw down a plate of food on my bedside table, then turned around and left. Kara had those eyes that didn't smile, even when her mouth was smiling. She and Tom never invited me to eat with them. My meals were always in my room, by myself. So I knew there was going to be a fourth foster home this year. When the caseworker from DCF came, I would tell her where I am a castaway for meals. But this family didn't know I would. They probably thought I would be too scared or shy. It wouldn't be long before I would grab the few things I had and throw them in a new garbage bag to take with me to the next home.

Trash Names

I learned to hate the terms "foster mother" and "foster father". These people were as far from being my mother or father as a porcupine is to a baby dolphin. Mothers and fathers should be about loving and caring for their children. But my caseworkers always referred to these families as my foster "mother", Joan or Dianne or Keisha or Carol. My foster "fathers" were Fred or Bill or Dave or Dion. Parents should have to earn the names of mother and father. Even I knew this. How could an adult social worker not know that? And I would move so often, how could I even have a chance at real parents?

Another thing about moving, I wish people would rename garbage bags and trash bags. Whenever they moved me, what little I owned would go into one. Not a suitcase or even a shopping bag. Always a trash bag. Maybe it was me they were throwing away.

Faded Paint

In my mind, I can go anywhere, do anything, have superpowers if I want. I'm pretty good at it, too. I like to imagine that someday I will have a small house on an island somewhere. I will sail to my heart's content. I don't like coming back to reality when I imagine things.

The walls in my room in this house were a moldy looking green color and faded except where old pictures used to hang. Just the darker squares and rectangles of paint. I stood in front of one dark rectangle and stared at it. I wondered for a long time what used to hang there, and then, instead of a picture, I imagined a movie in it's place. I saw a beautiful park, with a waterfall that flowed into the lake, and swings and a gazebo painted white. Families filled the grassy areas with blankets and picnic baskets. Dogs ran after the kids and played. The weeping willow trees that lined the lake tickled the air with their swaying, hanging branches. A pretty woman sitting on a bench looked over at me. She called my name.

"Joshua," she smiled.

It was my mother. She took my hand and led me to the swings, and we each got on. She was laughing, as her long hair swung behind her. I saw, off in the distance, sailboats on the still lake that had just enough of a breeze to fill their sails. My heart was light and warm, like the sun that draped us. I closed my eyes to let it bake on my face.

"What's wrong with you, fool?" Kara asked harshly as she entered my room while I was still staring at the wall. I didn't say a word. I just went over to my bed and sat down. She looked at my plate, which I hadn't touched and said,

"What a waste. I didn't cook this just to throw it out. It's cold now, but you're going to eat it anyway. In fact, you won't be getting another morsel until this is gone. And you better be up by six and go to school. I don't want another phone call from them asking where you are."

She has said this to me every night ever since I skipped school to go to my grandmother's funeral. She left the room and closed the door behind her. I laid my head down on my pillow. I wasn't hungry and I couldn't tell what the food in the plate was anyway, except for the instant mashed potatoes. When I knew they were asleep, I sneaked into the bathroom and flushed the food down the toilet. To me, that's the only thing that would be able to eat it.

The next morning, I got up before six, showered, dressed and left for school. No one else was up. They never got up for me and never made me breakfast. It didn't matter. It would have been too awkward for me to have to walk through a room with them in there anyway.

I walked quickly to school to avoid bullies which usually hung around places like fence breaks and alleys. Sometimes it was good to be in school, sometimes not. It depended on how well I could avoid certain boys that gave me a hard time. I got shoved around a lot by them, and since they were much bigger than me, I had to take it. Most schools I've been in have a zero tolerance policy, which is full of crap. If someone hit you and you tried to defend yourself, you were both suspended. If someone bullied you, you're supposed to go to the administrator and report it, which was equally stupid. Then they bring the students together and try to mediate the problem. Everyone knew if you report someone, after school you would get your ass kicked by the bully on the way home, or wherever else he could find you. It made it hard to go anywhere alone when there was no one who had my back. It was hard for me to make friends since I moved around so much. So I went to school as fast as I could, and returned home just as fast to my room. That was it. School and my room, every day, no matter where I lived so far.

When I was in my room one afternoon, I heard the doorbell ring. I looked down from my bedroom window and saw a lady with a briefcase. After being invited in, I could hear Kara in the living room talking to her. I heard her come up the stairs and knock on my door. She said a woman from DCF, which meant the Department of Children and Families, wanted to see me. I followed her downstairs.

"Hi Joshua," said the lady. "I'm your new caseworker. My name is Monica. How are you?"

I just looked at her. She is the fourth caseworker I've had. They come and go a lot. I guess I don't blame them. They always start out like they are going to change the world for you, and the longer they stay in their job, the more unhappy they look. Two out of the three I had before actually apologized to me about leaving. They said they didn't know the work was going to be so hard and they didn't have the heart for it. The other one just up and left without saying goodbye. I wish I could tell them what that felt like. Just when you start trusting someone, they up and leave your life. All that stays with me is my trash bag.

"Is everything okay?" she asked.

"No," I said. I could feel Kara's eyes pierce me.

"Why not?" Monica asked.

"They don't like me," I answered, my eyes directly challenging Kara's. "They don't even let me eat with them. I have to eat in my room, alone."

Monica looked at Kara who flustered out an excuse.

"Oh, you know how kids this age are. They misbehave, and if you send them to their rooms, they get angry. Of course he eats with us normally. It's just he skipped school, and he needed to know that won't be tolerated here. So he had to eat a meal in his room."

Monica looked back at me.

"You're lying," I said to Kara.

"And you are looking for another reason to have dinner in your room, young man," she snapped back.

She looked at Kara.

"I'm sorry this had to happen in front of you. He can be an angry young boy. But my husband and I are trying to be patient and talk to him to help him."

"Of course," Monica said. "May I see his room please?"

I led her up the stairs. When we got there, I tried again to tell her my plight. She looked at me, wrote something in her notes, and said,

"Well, everything seems to be okay, really. Maybe if you control your anger and be in school when you should, things will be better here. I'm going to leave my card with you, though. If you need to call, then please do. Try to work it out here, Joshua. You don't want to have to go to another home, do you?"

"Yes, I do. Please."

It was a losing battle. She wasn't going to believe me. That's how adults are. They believe each other and not us. We haven't learned to lie as well as they do yet. I always got caught when I tried to lie, so I know I am no good at it. Why keep trying something when it doesn't work? And what was the point in giving me her card? Kara was always home and a phone call to Monica wasn't going to happen anytime soon.

Monica descended the stairs, and I closed my door part way. I wanted to hear what they were saying to each other, but I couldn't make it out. I heard Monica speak briefly to Kara and then leave. I threw myself on my bed and covered my head with my pillow. I was angry now. Who would believe me? Who ever believed me? Probably no one.

Dragon Eyes

Shortly after he came in the house, Tom got into a yelling match with Kara. I heard him stomp loudly up the stairs to my room. He pushed my door open so hard, that it slammed into the wall behind it. I quickly jumped up. His face was fire engine red and his eyes were like flames. He grabbed me by the arm as he stripped off his belt and began to whip me with it. I yelled and screamed, but he screamed louder and kept at it. He told me if I ever told the social worker about eating in my room again, that this beating was nothing compared to the one I would get next time. I also realized that this is what Kara meant when she said Tom would let me "have it."

"You're a good for nothin' kid," he yelled. "Just keep ya trap shut, or I'll give you somethin' to keep it shut!" Then he stormed out, slamming the door behind him.

My skin was screaming. I could hardly make it back to the bed. I was shaking and nauseous. The stinging kept me from sleeping at all. I curled up on my bed, trying not to let the sheets or blanket touch my wounds. Hours of pain tortured my thoughts. My shower in the morning hurt my back and legs where his blows had landed. My skin was raw. I just wanted to get on my sailboat and leave, forever. But I had to figure out how to find land away from here, away from this nightmare. I will find a way today. I just knew it. I could feel it, like I could feel my legs and back stinging and my body still shaking.

I ran as well as my burning legs would take me when I left the house and headed straight for the sound. I grabbed my garbage bag to carry the few clothes I could stuff into it. I knew once I was on the boat it would be smooth sailing. Until then I kept my eyes peeled and didn't let anyone see me that knew me, even though I was scared someone would hear how loudly my heart was pounding.

I ran past the houses of people still waking up. I ran past the fields and a small farm. I saw the farmer leading a bull to plow the field. As I ran past, I thought about how his yoke looked heavy, like mine that brought me to my knees most days.

I could see the sound in the distance. I would be able to get on my sailboat nice and early and have all day to find a new land. My steps quickened as I got nearer and nearer, maybe two hundred yards away, where the dirt road with the aluminum buildings led to the docks.

"Hey, kid!" I heard someone yell.

I looked around and there was a cop getting out of his car which was parked in between the aluminum buildings.

"Hey, you!" he yelled again. "Stop right there!"

I walked faster. I was just beginning to see the whole shore. He began to follow me but there was no way I was going to stop. He started running and ordered me to stop. I didn't. There, at that dock, was my boat. He began to run fast and so did I. I had to make it to my boat. I just had to. I was so close. He was gaining on me. I felt him grab onto my bag over my shoulder and I let it slide into his hands. I could not let him get me. He tried to grab my arm, but I pulled away, just hard enough. He tried again, and this time he had a firm, tight grip.

He swung me around, held onto me tightly, and said,

"Kid, where are you going in such a hurry so early in the morning?"

I didn't answer. I knew he was going to send me back to Kara and Tom's house. I couldn't go back there.

"What's your name?"

Still panting from running, I looked at the ground.

"You need to come with me," he said, not letting go.

He walked me to his parked car and put me in the back. I noticed there were no handles on the inside of the back doors, so I could not even try to escape. He called the station and drove away from the sound. Away from my boat. Far away from another land.

When we got to the police station, he brought me inside and sat me at a desk.

"What's your name?" he asked as he sat back in his chair.

"Joshua," I replied.

"What's your last name?"

I ignored his question.

"Well, Joshua, wanna tell me where you live?"

He leaned forward and I looked at the floor.

"All right, then. How 'bout a soft drink, something to eat?" he asked.

I nodded. I hadn't had anything to drink or eat since yesterday at lunch.

"Hey Joe," he said to a younger cop. "Get this kid an orange juice and some peanut butter sandwich crackers from the vending machine, will ya?"

Joe got up right away and returned with the juice and crackers. I couldn't open the crackers and eat them fast enough.

"Whoa, slow down Josh. Might think you never ate. Listen, my name's Carl," the cop said. "I really would like to know where you were going. Wanna tell me?"

"Not really," I answered, even though he was trying hard to be nice to me.

"Why not?"

"Because no one ever believes me."

"Try me," he said.

I looked at him to see if he really meant what he said.

"No. You won't believe me."

"C'mon, kid. At least tell me your full name."

I was smart enough to know that was a trap. They would find out where I lived and return me there. I just wanted to get to my boat and leave. I had to figure out how to do that.

"Okay," he said. "Why don't you just tell me why you were heading for the docks? And I want the truth. Trust me. Cops are good at knowing when someone is lying. So if you tell me the truth, I will know it's the truth."

My welts were burning hot and I felt myself shaking. Before I could even think, I found myself blurting out,

"My foster father beat me really bad with his belt." I couldn't believe I said it, but I did. I felt my eyes start to water. Don't start crying, I told myself.

The cop looked at me. All 65 pounds of me. I wasn't sure if he believed me or not.

"When did that happen?" he asked.

"Last night."

"How badly are you hurt?"

He believed me.

I slowly rolled up my pant leg to my knee and showed him the welts. Then I showed him my back. He didn't say anything, but the look on his face said enough.

I told him what had happened.

"Please don't send me back there."

I saw Mike's mouth drop as he looked at my wounds. He paused and then said, "Don't worry, kid, we won't. Let's go take care of these welts. We have some antiseptic in our break room. C'mon. Come with me."

He sprayed my welts with something and it was cool and soothing. He was gentle with my clothes so they would not rub against them. He said he was going to help me get out of that house. He asked if he could take a couple of pictures of my welts, so he could file a report. I nodded my head.

"Now will you tell me your last name?"

I hesitated. "Jacobs," I told him.

He took a picture of my lower leg and one of my back, then went back to his desk. He told me to sit on a couch in the room we were in while he made some phone calls and typed things into his computer. After half an hour, he came over to me and said we were going for a ride.

"Where?" I asked.

"First, to the emergency room. I want a doctor to check you out. Then to a safe house for the rest of today and tonight. DCF will come by tomorrow and check on you and see what they can do to get you another place to live. I'm really sorry you had to go through this, kid."

"Me, too," I thought to myself.

The doctors asked me a lot of questions and took pictures of my wounds, too. Then they took some x rays. One heavy set nurse was very gentle when she dressed my welts and put ointment on them and covered them with gauze bandages. They still stung badly so they gave me some kind of painkiller and told Mike I would need Tylenol every four hours for a couple of days. My body felt weak and I was tired and just wanted to go to sleep. After five hours in the ER, Mike brought me to the safe house. There were other adults and some kids there. The safe house had a big living room in front that had couches and a desk in it. Mike stayed with me while the woman took some information from me and then from him.

"Joshua, my name is Cindy," she said. "We're going to keep you here for a while. At least until we can place you in another home."

That's not what I wanted to hear. I didn't want any more homes. They never worked out.

"Let's go get you settled," she said.

They walked me down a hallway to another room. It was even bigger than the room in front and had five bunk beds in it. Some of them had kids stuff on them, and some were empty.

"Pick an empty bunk for yourself," Cindy said.

I walked over to one and sat down.

"Have you eaten?" she asked.

"Not really," I said.

"Well, the bathroom is there." She pointed to a door. "Go and wash up and I'll show you where the kitchen is and we can make you something to eat. It'll be awhile before the other kids get back from school, but we have a TV room, if you'd like to watch something while you wait. I'll call your school and tell them you won't be in today."

I went to the bathroom and washed my hands. I came back out and Mike and the lady were talking, but stopped when they saw me return.

"I'm going to stop by your foster parents house and get the rest of your things and I'll bring them back here to you," Mike told me.

"You know where they live?" I asked.

"Yes, I do. But don't worry. They won't know where you are. They're going to be answering some serious questions, anyway, by the looks of you."

Good, I thought. I never wanted to see them again. I thought about my boat, but it was going to have to wait for now. Another day will come that I can sail away.

But I was too tired to deal with that right now. Cindy made a sandwich for me and then I went to my bunk, laid down and fell asleep.

Safe and Sound

I ended up staying at the safe house for two weeks, even though Monica came the next day to talk to me. She said she was sorry she did not believe me when she visited. It was too late for an apology. But I didn't say anything.

A special bus would come and pick up the other kids and me to take to each of our schools. The other kids were okay, but we all knew we were here for a reason. We told each other about some of the less serious things we went through, but only when the adults weren't around. The more serious things we kept to ourselves, though, under lock and key. Things we wanted to forget, things that hurt too deeply. Those were the secrets that would never be shared.

We ate together in a kitchen with a big table in it. We watched TV, played cards and some board games, and got our homework done. It wasn't so bad here. We couldn't play outside, but the first week was rainy anyway.

My twelfth birthday came and went with no one saying anything. No birthday wishes, no cake, no candles, no presents. It was like I didn't matter. I didn't exist. I felt empty and alone in the world. I was just a garbage bag stuck in a revolving door. One family to the next, like a bad dream. Hollow inside, like an echo. When I yelled from my internal anguish, the only voice that came back to me was my own. I wanted to have someone else's voice, anyone else's voice hear me and yell back. What made it worse sometimes was that when I felt like this and I couldn't control my crying, there was never a shoulder to bury my head on.

"Joshua," Cindy said one day, "we found a new home for you. This is a really nice family. They've had a lot of foster kids, and they all really liked them. Even the ones who aged out keep in touch with them."

Aging out was when you were too old for foster care anymore and you are pretty much on your own. Most times, it was 18, but I have known 16 year old's who aged out because they were either getting into too much trouble, or they quit school, or they ran away. I wanted to age out at 16, but I still had four years to go. Four years, when you are twelve, seems like eternity.

The next day, I put my three sets of clothes and my toothbrush into my garbage bag and Cindy and I drove to the new foster family's house. Driving up to it made my stomach turn in knots, especially not knowing what to expect. Cindy walked me up to the front door and rang the doorbell. A dog immediately started barking inside and I could hear people trying to calm him down. I wanted to throw up. A man and woman answered the door and welcomed us in. They had a golden retriever and I knew he was friendly as soon as he started wagging his tail.

The first room was a big living room, where other kids were playing a video game on the TV.

"Turn that off, kids, and come meet your new foster brother," the man said.

Four kids came into the room, three boys and a girl. Three were a little older than me, the girl was younger.

"Joshua, I'm Alex and this is my wife, Janet," the man said. "This is Michael, Jeremy, Corey and Kayla. Say hi to Joshua, kids."

They all said quiet hello's and looked at me probably like I was looking at them, scared and not knowing what to expect from each other. They huddled in one line across from me. Michael and Jeremy were white, maybe a little older than me, Corey was black, maybe my age and Kayla looked Hispanic and around five or six. Alex was tall and slender, with graying hair that he wore long, but combed back away from his face in a ponytail. He had glasses on and he looked a little nervous, but he looked happy. He had a suit jacket and jeans on with no tie, and an open shirt collar. Janet was a few inches shorter than him, and had a nice face with freckles. She had long red hair, but she wore it down. I don't ever think I have seen eyes as blue as hers before. She looked calm and when she smiled, her eyes did, too.

"Have a seat, please," Alex said to us as he motioned to the couch. "Let's get to know each other a little. Would you like a cold drink?"

I sat down next to Cindy. I put my bag on the floor next to me. I wasn't really listening to what Alex and Janet said because I was distracted looking around the room. It was a nice room. They had a lot of pictures of themselves with different kids, framed and sitting on tables or hanging on the walls. I think these must have been their other foster kids, but I had never been in a home before that had pictures like this. Maybe they are nice people, I thought, but I am not going to let my guard down yet.

"And so, since we could not have children of our own, and we love kids, we decided to be foster parents," I heard Alex say, as my ears tuned back into the conversation.

"So, Joshua, would you like to tell us a little bit about yourself?" Janet asked.

I didn't know what to say. Do they want to know my grandmother had died? Do they want to hear about all the foster homes I have been in? Did they want to know about being beaten and used, and how some kids bully me? Did they want to know how I have to run between houses and school to avoid certain kids? Did they want to know how hard it is for me to concentrate and why my grades were lousy? Or did they want to know what was in my garbage bag?

I just looked down at the floor, wishing I could blurt everything out, but not knowing them, I kept silent and just shrugged my shoulders.

"It's okay, Joshua, we can get to know each other in time," Janet said. "How about we take you around the house so you can begin to settle in?"

I looked at Cindy.

"I'll go with you if you want me to," she said. I nodded.

The house was bigger than I thought it would be. The kitchen was large with a table and plenty of chairs around it. The living room was large, too, with a TV bigger than any I had seen before. Video games were hooked up to it.

"You can play video games for an hour a day," Alex said. "We do homework together after dinner. I hope that works for you."

Works for me? No one ever offered that to me before. We went upstairs and there were four bedrooms. One was for Alex and Janet, one was for two of the boys, another small one was for the little girl, and the last one had two twin beds in it, one empty. I guess that one was for me.

"You can share this room with Corey," Janet said. "You can put your things in here, and there's a bathroom for you to share in the hall. Three of you can shower before bed and the other two in the morning. That way there is time for everyone to get ready before school."

"Pretty nice, isn't it?" Cindy asked me.

I nodded.

We went back downstairs and Cindy said it was time for her to go.

"I'll check in on you in a few days, Joshua, okay?" she said.

"Okay," I answered, now thinking it might be all right here.

She left and Corey asked me, "Do you play Madden NFL 11?"

"Not really," I answered.

"Well, come on. I'll show you how to play it."

I was not very good at it and I did not really know much about football, but Corey didn't seem to care. He said I'd get better at it once I played more.

It turned out that Alex and Janet were pretty nice people, after all. Alex leaves for work every morning to teach at the local college. Janet stays home and when we got back from school, she always had apples or bananas or cookies for us to snack on. She asked us about our day and everyone was anxious to tell her. When Alex got home from work, we had dinner and did homework around the kitchen table, just like they said we would. I began to feel like I was worth more than nothing, and that someone cared about how I did in school. I was behind in math and science, but Alex took extra time with me to catch up. It felt good. I was getting it and things were beginning to click in my head. I understood more and questioned more. I felt like I had been the last closed blossom on a plant, waiting for the right time to open, and the day had come.

On Sundays, we walked to the Baptist church a few blocks away. When we got there, people greeted Alex and Janet and they introduced us to people they knew. It was a very big church and was filled each Sunday. The pastor was the most handsome black man I have ever seen and has a smile that could light a night sky. When he preached his sermons, the congregation answered him. When the pastor really got going, it was like he was singing his sermon with perfect timing. People would throw their hands up and hold them there. AT first I thought it was funny watching them. Then I saw that they really felt what he was saying. The other kids and I began to go to Sunday school. I had never been before. They teach us about some stories in the Bible and how Jesus loves children. I wondered if He loves me and began to think He might. There were a lot of kids who wanted to play with us when the service was over. We ran around the grounds while the adults had coffee and food after church. Other adults began to recognize me and asked me how I was doing. For the first time in a long time, I began to feel like I mattered to other people. I decided I liked going to church. I felt at home there and that people really cared about me. Now I have a home and a place away from home that felt safe. Maybe there is no place like home.

At the house, we played lots of card and board games. Janet took us to the park after school on nice days and we played soccer or went on the swings and jungle gym. I felt normal for the first time in my life and for the first time I could remember, it felt like I belonged to a real family. I want to stay with this family forever. Even the dog, Romeo, and I play in the yard every day. I never had it so good. And Corey was right. I got better at video games.

Three months went by and we were getting ready for Christmas. The first Christmas tree I can recall was put in the living room. We helped decorate and string the lights on it. Alex and Janet put wrapped presents under the tree, with our names on various ones.

Wow, I thought, I'm going to get a Christmas present this year. I wanted to give everyone a present, too, but I had no money. Then one day, Alex had us pile into the van and we went to the mall. Alex sat down in front of us and gave each of us forty dollars. He said, "Go buy each other some presents to put under the tree. Just keep them in the bags, so no one can see what you got for them."

This meant we had ten dollars to spend on each person, except Alex and Janet. They said they had enough presents, and there was no need to get them anything. Ten dollars each wasn't much money for a present, but it was more than I ever had all at once.

"We'll keep Kayla with us, and you boys can meet us back here at the clock tower in an hour, so you can do your shopping in secret," Janet said. "Okay?"

"OK," we all said in unison and took off in different directions.

"Remember... one hour! That means five o'clock!" Janet yelled again as we ran off.

I went into a store that had small gifts. I found a lot of things under ten dollars in here. I picked out things that I thought would go with the personalities of each of my foster brothers and sisters. I can't remember ever feeling so good next to being on my sailboat. I was happy for the first time in my life.

About one week before Christmas, we all made a gingerbread house. It turned out kind of sad looking because none of us had done this before, but we didn't care. I never knew I loved gingerbread. The spicy scent that rose from it, and then dipping the pieces into a glass of milk was like a dream. We cleaned up and went to bed. I was really tired and fell asleep fast. Before I did, though, my sailboat popped into my head. Thinking about it happened less and less. I wondered if it was still where I had left it, but it didn't seem to matter that much anymore. The sound was about three miles from where I lived now. I thought about asking Alex to take me there one day to check on it, but I never seemed to get around to it.

I woke to Romeo barking and pulling off my blanket.

"Romeo, stop," I kept telling him. But he kept at it. "What's wrong with you?" I yelled at him. He kept barking.

When I began to smell smoke, and saw it creeping under the bedroom door, I sat up. I jumped up and woke Corey.

"Wake up, Corey!" I yelled. I jumped out of bed and shook him. "I think the house is on fire! Get up!" I ran into the hallway full of smoke. "Alex! Janet! The house is on fire!" I started coughing, but found my way into their bedroom.

"Wake up!" I yelled again. "The house is on fire! "They bolted out of bed, grabbing me to go with them.

"Get outside with them!" Alex yelled to Janet and us when we got to the staircase. "I'll get the other kids and Romeo."

Romeo was barking nonstop. Alex ran to the other bedrooms, coughing hard, while Janet, Corey and I ran downstairs. The tree was on fire and we could feel the heat from it from the staircase. We turned for the front door, choking, eyes burning, then Janet grabbed us and pushed us ahead of her. We got to the front door and onto the porch. We were bent from coughing and trying to breathe. Where was Alex? Were he and the other kids going to make it out?

Janet pulled us to the yard and turned to look back at the house, anxious for Alex, Kayla and Jeremy to come. We heard Alex calling for Romeo, who was barking like crazy, but he wouldn't leave until everyone was out. Just as Alex, with Kayla in his arms, Jeremy, Michael and Romeo got out, a window burst and shattered into a million pieces. Janet turned to cover us with her body.

We ran to the sidewalk, well away from the house and stood there shocked while the flames consumed the downstairs and watched how the upstairs began to explode in fire. Alex ran to the neighbor's house to call the fire department.

By the time they got there, the house was fully in flames. It took them hours to get it under control. It was a blackened, cracked, and smoldering skeleton when they turned off the hoses to check for any more flames. No one knew what started it. The fire marshal told Alex he was going to have to investigate what happened, but said he had a feeling it started near the Christmas tree, possibly a short in the wire of lights or the outlet. The house was older, but not that old. He said it may take awhile to know for sure, maybe a few days. The EMT's checked each one of us. Alex breathed through an oxygen mask for a while, then he threw up. They told him he should go to the emergency room, but he insisted he was okay. He had breathed in the most smoke out of all of us. He sat on the stone wall near the sidewalk, trying to recover. I sat next to him and put my hand on his arm.

"You gonna be okay?" I asked him.

"Sure, son. No problem. I just need a minute."

That was the first time anyone called me "son." It made a warmth run through me, even though we had just had a horrible thing happen.

When there were only some smoldering beams, the firemen packed up their things. The fire marshal stayed behind with us. Alex was shaken, like the rest of us, but he was talking to the marshal and no one wanted to interrupt. He walked over to us when he was through, and told us to get in the van, which had been parked on the street. We drove to a hotel to stay for the rest of the night.

"My God," was all Janet could seem to say as she kept turning her head so we would not see her tears.

Alex held her hand while he drove. We were all silent and in disbelief. Kayla was crying quietly in her car seat and Janet tried to soothe her by reaching for her cheek. Where would we live now? What would happen to us?

Alex was trying to be strong, even I could tell. He kept looking at us through the rear view mirror. When we got to the hotel, he went in and checked in while we waited in the car.

"We'll get this figured out tomorrow, kids," he told us when he returned. "Let's try and regroup and get some rest. Come on, let's go find our suite."

It was Saturday, so none of us had to go to school or work the next day. Janet was crying quietly and I felt bad for her. She probably lost everything she had. And all those presents we bought for each other, gone. The gingerbread house, the Christmas tree, the video games, all gone. But Romeo saved us. I was proud of him. I slept on the fold out couch with Corey and tried to sleep. Romeo jumped in with us. Everything that just happened kept running through my head. If it wasn't for Romeo, we never would have made it out of the house. Maybe that's why people say dogs are a man's best friend.

The next day, we went to Friendly's for breakfast. When we finished ordering, Alex and Janet told us they had to talk to us about something serious.

I watched as Alex swallowed and his Adam's apple bobbed up and down in his neck.

"Kids," he began, "Our insurance company is going to cover rebuilding our house. But that's going to take several months to do, maybe longer. In the meantime, they are going to put Janet and I in a hotel with a kitchen and living room. They won't cover the money it will cost for all of you to stay there, and unfortunately we don't have that kind of money. So, just until the house is ready to live in again, DCF is going to put you in other foster homes. But it's only while we rebuild the house. Then you can come back to us. We promise. No matter what, you will come back to us. We love you all and want you with us. It's just going to be awhile before we can have you back. Hang in there and be patient. We will come and get you."

"Yes, we will," Janet added.

For the first time, I saw tears run down from Corey's eyes.

My stomach sank. It wasn't bad enough that the house burned down, and that we weren't going to have Christmas, but now we had to go live somewhere else and probably not together. Alex and Janet kept talking, but I drifted away to think about my sailboat again. Maybe I would sail around the world this time. It wouldn't matter if I couldn't find land, because I would stay at sea. No one would be able to find me or catch me because the sea is so huge. When I got back, it would be just in time to move back into Alex and Janet's new house, if they remembered me by then. I'm glad I never asked Alex for that ride to the sound to check on my boat, and because I never brought it up, he never knew about it in the first place. I think that no matter where I go, my boat would have to be a secret only to me. A kid never knows what tomorrow might hold.

Keeping My Head Above Water

It isn't like I am a troublemaker. Trouble found me, no matter where I went. Sometimes I think that darkness follows me like a shadow. Or maybe like a shadow in the dark. You can't really see it, but it's there, even with the tiniest of light.

On Monday, Cindy came and got us and brought us back to the safe house. We had to stay here again until they could find homes for us. We were still together, but we missed Alex and Janet. I was having a hard time sleeping. I kept picturing Romeo pulling the blankets off of me in such detail, that each time I began to drift off to sleep, I caught myself picking my head up and looking to see if he was there. Then I would see the house falling in on itself, flames unsatisfied no matter how much of the house they swallowed.

Going to sleep Christmas eve was like all the rest I remembered, not exciting like I had imagined it only a week ago. I woke up the next morning and went into the kitchen where Cindy was making coffee and a couple other people were cooking.

"Good morning, Joshua. Merry Christmas," Cindy said. Why wasn't she with her family, I thought.

"Merry Christmas," I said.

"This is Leonard and Martha. Leonard and Martha, this is Joshua," Cindy said.

"Merry Christmas," they said together.

"You, too," I said back.

"They've come to help make Christmas dinner for all of us. It's going to be a great meal. Go wash up and see if anyone else is up. Then we could use your help in here."

I wasn't very excited about helping and it must have shown on my face.

"Go on," Cindy said. "You'll see. It'll be fun."

I returned to the kitchen cleaned up, but no one else was awake yet. Cindy brought a large bowl to the kitchen table and placed it in front of me. I looked inside it and saw a large mound of light brown dough with chocolate chips in it.

"Your job is to make the chocolate chip cookies for dessert," Cindy said. "Just scoop some batter up like this, and drop them on the cookie sheet in rows. See?" she showed me. "Just like that. Try to get them the same size so that they cook evenly."

I slowly began my task. Trying to get the balls of dough the same size made me take my mind off of other things. I looked at her while she mixed stuffing with her bare hands next to me.

"Why aren't you with your family today?" I asked her.

"Because I wanted to be with you," she said as she touched a dollop of stuffing on the tip of my nose.

"Hey!" I laughed as I wiped it off with my sleeve.

"No, really," I said. "Why are you here and not with them?"

"Well, my young man," she began, "I'm like you. I have no family to speak of. I've been an orphan my whole life. I went from home to home, but no one ever wanted me forever."

"Like me?"

"In some ways, yes," she said.

"So how did you become a caseworker? Didn't you have to go to college or something?" I asked, puzzled because I never thought about college or that I would ever go to one. I just wanted my life to be my own and aging out couldn't happen too soon for me.

Cindy said, "Well, when I graduated from high school, I got a job at a local pharmacy. I worked very hard because I had to pay my own rent and my own bills. I was the only one I could depend on. The woman who was the pharmacist, Rose was her name, took a liking to me and often invited me to her house for Sundays and holidays. Rose had no children of her own and her husband had passed away a few years before. I guess she was lonely. I told her my dreams of going to college, but that it would be a very long time before I could afford to go. She was always interested in me and how I was getting along in life." I imagined that Alex and Janet would be the same way to me.

"One Christmas," she continued, "Rose handed me an envelope, which of course, I assumed was a Christmas card. It was, but then I saw there was a handwritten note in it and a check. She gave me the tuition for my first semester at City College. She said if I kept a 3.5 average, which is like a low A to you, she would keep paying tuition for me until I got my Master's degree in the field of my choice. I couldn't believe my eyes, or my gift. That was the most amazing thing anyone has ever done for me. Like a miracle. I knew I wanted to do social work, so that's what I majored in. I was so focused on my work, I graduated with a 3.86. And that," she winked, "is why I am here today."

I had never thought about an adult being an orphan like me. I had never met one before. Cindy wanted to spend Christmas with us, it was not like she had to or was obligated to. It made me feel good inside.

The rest of the day we all enjoyed a turkey dinner, the tree, and it turned out to be a better day than I thought. Cindy and the other adults played charades with us and a couple of board games. After dessert, Leonard sat down at the old upright piano against the wall that was barely ever touched, and began to play. Cindy sang along with him and eventually we all joined in, once we got over being shy about it. I went to bed feeling a little bit of happiness trying to take over the longing I had forever felt in my heart. It took over just long enough for me to smile as I closed my eyes. There were no pictures of the fire in my head that night.

Zero Tolerance

It was several weeks before each of us were placed in new homes and I was the last to go. Cindy drove me to a house not far from the safe house.

"Well, Joshua, this is your new temporary home for now," she said.

Once inside, it was a lot different from Alex and Janet's house. It was pretty messy and there were four-year-old twin boys. From the looks of things, I think they were the cause of much of the mess.

"Hey kid, how ya doin'?" a very large woman named Mary who promptly sat down in an easy chair said to me. "That's Johnnie and that's Joseph." She pointed to each of the boys.

"Well, come here. Let me get a good look atcha."

I took one step forward.

"I don't bite," she continued. "C'mere,"

I took a few steps closer. She was really big. So big, I thought if she stood up, the chair might come with her. Her eyelids fell in folds over her eyes so only the pupils showed.

"Well, aren't you a handsome one?"

I had never thought about being handsome. I was just a kid. Are kids handsome?

Cindy looked at my room, stayed for about an hour, and then she left.

Mary was still sitting in her chair and asked me to go to the kitchen and get some cookies from the counter for the boys and me. I began to wonder if she ever got up out of that chair. I just wanted to leave. I didn't want to be here with two little boys and this lady. Then she said her husband would be home soon and I could meet him. I didn't want to meet him. I was tired and just wanted to go to "my" room and sleep. But I had to feel things out here, first.

She asked me some things about myself and I was giving her one word answers. She was messy, like she didn't shower or something. She wore what looked like a big flowery cotton sheet that had a hole in it for her head to fit through and two others for her arms.

"Put those puzzle pieces back in the box, would you, Josh?" she said to me.

"And while you are up, grab these cups and dishes and put them in the kitchen sink. I don't want this place lookin' like this when Howard gets home."

I guessed Howard was her husband. But why was she asking me to do these things? I just got here. Why wasn't she doing anything except sitting in her chair?

The two boys were sitting on the couch watching Sesame Street. I sat down next to them. There didn't seem to be anything else to do.

After another half hour, Mary got up very slowly off the chair and told me she was going to go in the kitchen and make some dinner.

"Mac and cheese for dinner tonight," she said. "Stay here with the boys while I cook."

A man showed up at 5:30.

"Hi. I'm Howard. You must be the new kid."

I nodded. He came closer to me and stood over me for a minute.

"I smell mac and cheese," he said. "Same old. Oh, well, at least Mary adds some things to the box mix to make it better."

He was a tall man with a big belly and had a broad back and big, thick hands. He sat down in another easy chair and looked toward the kitchen. "Mary," he shouted. "I'm home."

We ate on the couches and chairs in the living room. The boys stood at the coffee table and scooped their dinners from bowls with spoons when they took occasional breaks from playing. After dinner, I told Mary I was tired and was going to bed.

"Bring Johnnie and Joseph up with you," she said. "Put them in their beds. Johnnie, Joseph, c'mon. Joshua is going to put you to bed. Josh, make sure they brush their teeth."

I had one boy in each hand as I ascended the stairs. We went into the bathroom and we all brushed our teeth. I put them in their beds and told them to go to sleep. They started horsing around, got out of bed, and began playing with some toys in there.

"Get back in bed," I said to them, picking them up, one by one and laying them down. "Go to sleep."

They started to giggle, but I was too tired to deal with them, so I closed their door as I left to go to my room.

The next morning I got ready for school. When I got downstairs, Mary was fast asleep in her now reclined easy chair. She must have slept there all night. She opened her eyes, looked at me and said,

"Mornin'. You can go make yourself a sandwich for lunch. There's paper lunch bags in the cupboard next to the fridge. If you're hungry now, there's cereal in there, too."

She didn't get up to help, so I just went in the kitchen and had some cereal, then made a sandwich for lunch.

I was going to a different school this time, where I would know no one. It was pretty big for a middle school. I went into the office to tell them I was here. The secretary, Mrs. Conners, wrote down some information and said she was going to assign another student to help me get around. She handed me my class schedule and then I took a seat and waited. Within a few minutes, a kid who looked like an eighth grader came over to me and said,

"Hi. I'm Andrew. Are you Josh?"

"Yeah," I answered.

"Okay. I'm gonna show you around, then I'll take you to your first period class. Come on. We can go through here."

I followed him through the back door of the office that led into a hall. He showed me where the auditorium was, the cafeteria, the art rooms, the music rooms, and then walked me to my first period class.

Before he left, he said, "Just ask anyone in there where to find your next class. Most likely many of them will have the same schedule as you, so it'll be easy. Okay?"

"Okay. Thanks," I said.

It was never easy walking into a new school, never mind walking into a class late, because everyone stares at you. According to my schedule, this was a science class. I went in and handed the teacher my schedule. All the kids were looking at me.

"Welcome, Josh. Everyone, this is Josh," he said. "He's new here, so let's let him know how welcome he is."

"Hi, Josh," some of the kids muttered.

"Pick any empty desk to sit at," the teacher said.

The teacher turned to write something on the board, and when he did, someone in the back of the class threw a wadded up piece of paper at me and it bounced off of my head. A few kids giggled as I took a seat.

I looked at some of the other kids. One boy was making faces at me. A girl smiled at me. Another was drawing cartoon faces and another was taking notes. I got a notebook and pencil out of my backpack and tried to pay attention. The class was noisy and the teacher seemed to just muddle along, shuffling through papers on his desk, writing on the chalkboard, ignoring small missiles flying past him. My next few classes weren't much different. Then it was lunch time.

The cafeteria had two long lines of kids who were buying lunch. I took my bagged lunch and went into the outdoor area, where there were a bunch of picnic tables. I picked an empty one under a tree and sat down and pulled out my sandwich. Mary didn't give me any money to buy a drink, which I would have liked to have had. As I was eating, a group of boys came over to me and stood staring at me.

"Hey, nerd," the bigger one said, with his arms crossed in front of him.

I just continued eating.

"Hey, I was talking to you," he said. "Are you ignoring me? Who said you could sit here?"

"No one," I answered.

"I didn't think so," he said, as he snatched my sandwich away from me and threw it into the gravel on the ground.

"Next time, ask," he commanded.

I got up and stared at him.

"Don't do that again," I said.

"Aw. Little kid wants his sandwich. Gonna cry?"

"I said don't do that again."

"What are ya gonna do about it?"

It was times like these that turned me into someone I didn't recognize, times that confused me between being a boy and a man, or maybe a boy and an animal. It was like a hot feeling that began in my feet and rose up through my body. I could feel it coming and I had no control over it. It stiffened me at first, logic battling anger, sanity battling insanity. I could feel my hands turn into fists, white knuckled and tight. I punched him as hard as I could in the stomach. The next thing I knew, we were on the ground fighting. A few teachers broke their way through the gathering crowd of kids, who were cheering on the fight, and pulled us away from each other, both of us still struggling to get in one more punch. We walked to the principal's office, me, trying to calm myself, but still angry inside.

Great, I thought, once I calmed down. In trouble on my first day.

The principal was a big man with broad shoulders and glasses. His name was Mr. White. He told us to sit down in the chairs in his office and wait for him while he spoke to a teacher outside of his office, presumably about us. The other kid was snickering at me while we waited.

Then he said, "You're dead."

I glared at him, wishing my eyes were bullets piercing him.

Mr. White walked in and sat down on his chair.

"I am going to ask you boys to answer my questions one at a time," he said sternly. "All right, Mr. Jacobs. This is your first day here and you're already fighting. Zach, you are not new here, and this is the third time you have been in my office this year alone. So Jacobs, what happened out there?'

"Nothing," I said. I wasn't going to rat, even on my enemy. I found this out in fourth grade. You rat, you pay.

"Well, something must have happened or you wouldn't have fought," Mr. White said. "Okay. Zach, what do you have to say?"

"He just got up and punched me in the stomach while I was walking by," the liar said.

"I would find that hard to believe," Mr. White said to him. "It's his first day here. He doesn't know you. Why would he pick you out of a crowd of students, and punch you? And besides that, you are bigger than him."

"I don't know," Zach shot back. "Ask him."

Mr. White looked at me.

"Josh?"

I couldn't keep myself from glaring at Zach. I glanced at Mr. White and then back to glaring at Zach. I kept my mouth shut.

"Okay. I can see we are not going to get anywhere here," Mr. White said. "So I will be calling both of your homes and letting your parents know what happened. In the meantime you are both suspended for 10 days. Josh, I know that's tough on your first day here, but that is our policy. Zero, and I mean zero tolerance. Your teachers will be sending your daily work to my office and your parents can pick it up. You are expected to hand it in when you get back."

Like that's going to happen, I thought to myself.

"Now you boys go sit outside my office while I call your parents, and keep your hands and your comments to yourselves, unless you want to be suspended further."

I sat with my arms crossed with my head against the wall and closed my eyes. If I could just get to my boat. I daydreamed about being on it, a nice warm summer day with the wind billowing the sail, and my fingertips skimming the smooth water below. I also thought about Cindy. About how well she did in school and became what she wanted to become. I blew my chances for that on my first day here.

It was interrupted by Mr. White

"Zach, your mother is on her way to pick you up. Joshua, your mother can't get here, so you will sit here until the end of the school day and take the bus home."

"She's not my mother," I murmured under my breath.

When I got home, Mary was waiting in her chair.

"Want to explain yourself and what happened today?"

I shook my head.

"Then go up to your room and think about it and if you want to come explain yourself, you can. And no dinner tonight for you."

That's just great, I thought. No lunch, no dinner. My stomach was growling. I went to the bathroom and got a long drink of water, sticking my mouth under the faucet. I learned a long time ago that water can make you feel full, at least for a little while. I laid down on my bed and soon fell asleep even though my stomach was growling. Sleeping was another way to escape the feelings of hunger.

When I woke up, I realized there was nothing but a deck of cards on the night table to occupy my time. I began to build a house of cards, imagining it to be my real house when I found an island one day.

I heard Howard come home. He didn't come upstairs. Well into the night, I heard him ascend the stairs and knock on my door.

"Come in," I said.

He came in and sat down on the bed while I was putting the finishing touches on my island house.

"Have somethin' you wanna talk about?" he asked.

"No."

"You know why you're here, Josh?"

"Yes."

"I don't think you do."

I looked at him. Of course I knew why. Because Alex and Janet's house burned down.

"You're here because no one else wants you."

Alex and Janet wanted me.

"You're here because every house you go to, you cause trouble and you get kicked out. You're a troublemaker. Now you've been suspended. See, kid, not even the school wants you. So we're stuck with you now. And you're gonna do as we say. As I say. Stand up and come over here."

I got up and walked to him.

"I think you need to learn a lesson, kid."

I was waiting for him to pull off his belt, and then I would hightail it out of there.

"Pull your pants down," he commanded.

"What?"

"You heard me. Pull your pants down."

"No."

He grabbed my arm. His strong, thick hands were hurting my arm.

"You see, Mary and I are the only ones who are gonna take care of you now. So you are gonna do as I say. Now pull your pants down." I stared at him with defiance. "Do it," he commanded as he grabbed my arm with his big thick hand.

I realized I had no choice. He was much bigger than me. Mary never got out of her chair downstairs, so she was no help. I didn't know why he wanted me to do this. I guess he was going to beat my butt.

I pulled my jeans down to my ankles.

"Boxers, too," he said.

I began to feel really sick. If I had had anything in my stomach, I would have puked it out right then and there. I couldn't swallow. I could feel my breathing getting short.

"Do it," he commanded again.

"No," I answered.

"If you don't, my belt might be the answer."

I reached for my boxers and slowly let them drop. I had never stood naked like this in front of a man before. I could feel my cheeks flush.

What happened next, I can't put into words. Well, I could, but I can't write them down. If I did, it would make it too real, and I don't want that. Written words would take it from something I will always try to block, to something I would have to bring into the real world. What he did to me wasn't a natural thing. It was humiliating, painful, and bloody. His hand covered my mouth and kept me from screaming, even though I wanted to the whole time. I couldn't walk right for two days. Mary asked me what was wrong with me. I was too scared to tell her. I wish I could get what happened out of my head. But I can't. It comes to me in the strangest moments, like right in the middle of math class or something like that. I can't concentrate. I wanted to kill someone and I wanted to die. I wanted to tell someone to get me out of there, but I knew I would never be able to because I could not say the words, either. I felt like I was becoming invisible. I was completely alone. No one wanted me, no one cared about me. I was twelve now, and my life was already over.

I began to have sit-right-up-in-bed-sweating nightmares. I usually could not fall back to sleep and would only sleep in short spurts during the day, when Howard was at work. Mary never went to pick up my homework, but she had plenty of chores for me to do. I had to clean up after the boys, wash dishes, put the garbage out, vacuum, dust, clean the two and a half bathrooms, make breakfast and lunch for the boys, and whatever else that kept her from having to get out of her chair. When she would fall asleep when the boys took their naps, I would, too. I was always tired from listening for Howard at night.

M.I.A.

When I was finally back at school, we had to use our classroom computers for research. I sat at one and began to type "Jackson Jacobs" in Google search; my father's name. I had to find him. He was my last hope for rescuing me. I knew, no matter where he was, he would come and get me to save me from all of this. His name came up many times, and I decided to click on the first one. I was so focused on what would be there, I didn't notice my teacher, Miss Johnson, come up behind me.

"Joshua, what are you doing?" she said.

I quickly closed the window, and responded, "Uhm, nothing, Miss."

"Get back to what you are supposed to be doing, young man. If I catch you doing something on the computer that was not assigned to you, you will be sent to the office."

I didn't need that again.

At least I knew my father was out there. Maybe I could get to the public library in town and find him with their computers. Then I wouldn't have someone watching behind me. The only problem is getting there. It's four miles away from where I live now. So is the sound where my sailboat is.

Nights Sweats

I wasn't sleeping much anymore. My sleep was more like a ten minute doze and then I would wake up in cold sweats. I kept thinking, is he going to come into my room again? Is he going to come in here and do that horrible thing to me? How would I get away? Where would I go? Who would I be able to tell? No one. I am stuck here.

Then I remembered that Monica had given me her card. I hope I still have it. Maybe there is some way I can tell her. Maybe she will come to visit soon. How will I explain it to her? How will I be able to make a phone call without Howard and Mary finding out? What will happen to me if they do? How am I going to get away from here?

Julie

A week passed and Howard didn't bother me. At school a girl named Julie sat with me at lunch. She was in two of my classes. She looked sad.

"Hi, Josh," she said. "Mind if I sit with you?"

"Go ahead," I said.

She sat quietly and I thought I saw her eyes watering up, but I didn't know what to say.

The silence was awkward, so I finally said the only thing that came to mind. "So, uhm, do you like it here?"

"I did until this morning," she said.

"What happened this morning?"

"Just some girls I thought were my friends. They aren't, turns out."

"How do you know?"

"Because I told them something in private and now the whole school knows."

I didn't know what she was talking about.

"I didn't hear anything," I told her.

"Well, girls are mean," she said. "One week they are your friends and the next they are your enemies."

I knew that was kind of true, at least in middle school. I would see some girls hanging out together like best friends, and the next time I saw them, they were fighting and saying mean things to each other. Sometimes they would get into fights that were worse than boys' fights. They would grab each other's hair and try to yank it out of their heads. They had nails, too.

"And this isn't the first time this has happened. I should have learned. Guys aren't so mean. I think I am going to have only boys for friends from now on," she told me.

I wasn't so sure that guys were not mean, they could be mean in other ways, but I found myself hoping I could be one of her friends because she seemed nice. It was hard for me to make friends because of all the schools I have been to and it was hard for me to trust anyone.

"Hey, Josh," she said. "Want to walk home after school with me?"

"Okay," I said, not ever having this kind of offer before, especially from a girl. "Where do you live?'

"On Maple Ave. It's only a few blocks from here."

I thought how great this would be. I wouldn't have to go to Howard and Mary's right after school. I had somewhere else to go and someone to go with. We finished lunch, and she told me where to meet her after school. I was glad I had something else to think about.

Julie was waiting under the tree, right where she said she'd be after school.

We walked and talked. Actually she did most of the talking, and I was glad about that because I really didn't know how to talk to girls. She made me feel relaxed, though. She told me about her family and which teachers she liked and didn't like.

Her house was a large Victorian, set far back from the street, with the biggest front porch I have ever seen with rocking chairs on it and a few tables between them. There were huge trees in her yard that blocked the view from the street and made it feel like we were someplace special.

"I'm just going to let my mom know I'm home, and then we can hang out if you want."

"Okay," I said.

I sat down in one of the rockers. It really was peaceful there.

She returned a few minutes later with some cookies and two glasses of lemonade. Man, they tasted good. She sat in another rocker.

"So, Josh, what about you? Where do you live?"

That was something I did not want to tell her.

"A few blocks away from the other side of school," was all I was willing to share. She was good with that.

"Did you see Joe's face in science class today when he got caught texting on his cell phone?"

Texting in class was a big rule breaker. Especially when we were having a test. The teachers assume we were cheating, would take the phone away, and we got a big fat zero on the test. That's what happened to Joe. Then they call your parents and you can't have your phone back until one of them comes to get it from the principal. We all knew what that meant.

"Yeah, he got in a lot of trouble," I said.

"Well, that was a stupid move."

We talked and giggled the afternoon away. It felt good to have a friend. It took my mind off of other things that I did not want to think about.

When I noticed the sun creeping near the tops of the trees, I decided I'd better get home before dark fell. I didn't want to, but I had nowhere else to go.

On my way, I came up with a plan. I decided I was going to put the dresser in my room against the door at night since it would not lock. I wondered why I hadn't thought of this before. Great idea, I told myself.

"Where have you been?" Mary asked when I walked in.

"I was at a friend's house," I answered, not knowing how she would take that.

"Who told you that you could do that?"

"No one," I answered meekly.

"Well, you need to come straight home from school from now on," she snapped back at me. "I need you here. You think taking care of all of you is easy?"

Taking care of all of us? She hardly did anything. I was her slave, pretty much.

"You have a lot of chores to do. Now get in the kitchen and clean it up in there."

I put my backpack down and did what she said. When I was done, she had me clean up the living room floor from all the toys the twins had left around. Then she told me to go to my room and she would call me for dinner. Mac and cheese. Again.

After dinner, she and Howard had me clean up the dishes. Then I told them I had to go do my homework.

"Good night," I said, wanting them to think I would do my homework and then go to sleep.

I went to my room and walked over to the dresser. It was just a little shorter than me and I tried to shake it a little to see how heavy it was. It was heavy. It would keep my door shut, though. Trying to move it would be hard. I decided to take the drawers out, one by one, move the dresser, and then put the drawers back. I had to be quiet about it, too. I would be fine until morning. I would have to get up a little early to move the dresser back to where it was, but it was going to become my fortress at night. My fortress against Howard. After I got the drawers out, I tipped it at each corner and put a tee shirt under each leg, then pushed it slowly across the wood floor to the door and put the drawers back in. It took me awhile, especially since I did not want them to hear me downstairs. I felt safe now. I felt I was beginning to have some control over protecting myself and what happened to me. I needed more of that. I laid down, content with my plan, and fell into the deep sleep I needed to have.

I woke to a hand over my mouth. A big, strong hand. Howard was standing over me and when I looked to the door, it had been opened with the dresser right behind it, pushed aside.

"Think you were going to keep me out?" the voice whispered.

I tried to struggle, but he was too strong for me. He grabbed at my underwear and I twisted my face away from his hand and screamed. I began to fight him and he smacked me hard with the back of his hand, his ring slamming into my cheek. I felt like I was going to pass out. He latched onto my thigh and flipped me over. I shook off the dizziness. I shook off the weakness. I shook off the powerlessness, twisted away and screamed as loud as I could. Anger enveloped me in one huge grip. I felt the adrenaline steam through my body and I used it to fight. This wasn't going to happen anymore, not to me. I lashed punches at him with both hands, missing their target each time. He grabbed both of my wrists with one hand and held them secure. I tried to twist away. It was no use. He was too strong for me. I closed my eyes tight, still struggling with everything in me. I could feel the weight of his body on the bed. He let his hand go from my mouth and I gave one final scream. He covered my mouth again, even harder. I was in survival mode, but losing the battle. I felt his heavy body climbing on me. I was done for. There was no way out. I struggled and struggled, but was pinned like a fly in a spider web. Suddenly I heard a sound like a loud clang. His body landed on me with a dead weight, and his hands let go completely. I opened my eyes and there, standing over his body on mine, was Mary, cast iron skillet in hand, breathing hard, anger and shock in her tearing eyes. Mary, who never came upstairs, who rarely left her chair, found her way to me. She pushed his body off of mine and it landed on the floor with a thud. She reached for my hand, pulled me off the bed, walked me out the door and slammed it closed, with her husband lying dead on the floor. She said nothing as she walked me down the stairs into the living room. When we got there, she sat down on her chair, still holding my hand, looked at me and said,

"Call the police."

Waking Up

After the police came and arrested Mary, they took me to the hospital. The police questioned me for a long time. All I really wanted to know was where Mary was. I wanted to hug her, to thank her and never stop. I wanted to know she was safe and no one was going to hurt her. I wanted Carl, the cop who helped me, to be with her. I wanted to talk to him, tell him to take care of her and tell him how she saved me. I wanted him to protect her. Where was he? My question went unanswered. And when they finished, I got taken once again, to the safe house. Cindy hugged me tight when she saw me.

I thought about Mary a lot. The person who never did much of anything, never got out of her chair, even to sleep, saved me. What she must have done to climb those stairs. Days later, I thought she must have climbed them twice. Once to see what was happening and again to get the skillet, but I will never know and never wanted to ask her. She must have known if she did not come prepared, she could not have helped me. She must have found her line between selfishness and selflessness. Maybe he had been mean to her. Maybe there was a past between them that found its last straw. All I do know is that she rescued me from horror and she rescued my life, risking her own.

My sailboat was unreachable for me now, if it was even still there. It had been so long since I had checked on it, I wondered if it was washed to sea, or stolen. It would serve me right, since I stole it to begin with. I had no transportation and no money. I was safe, but alone again. But being alone this time was different. I began to believe that some people like Mary, like Alex, like Janet would protect me. People like Mary were not the lazy people I thought they were. Alex and Janet saved my life, too, in more ways than they might ever know. The fire was not their fault. I began to realize that adults were not how I had thought about all of them, and that some people are good inside, even if I had judged the outside. Maybe I could be like them someday. Maybe I could help kids like me and do what Cindy does. Maybe now I had something to look forward to and that some people did care about me. I felt older now.

Months passed, but each month I would go and visit Mary in jail. The jury had decided she had gone too far to protect me, but I think she did just fine. I told her so. She got three years and could get out in one with good behavior. She didn't seem to mind. She even said it was worth it. That I, Joshua Jacobs, was worth it. I hugged her each time I left and told her I would never forget her, that she was my hero, and that I would visit her when she got out of jail, too. She just sat in her seat and held my hand on the table.

"You're a good kid, Joshua," she said. "I know I was a lazy old coot, and I was hard on you, but that didn't mean I didn't care."

That might have been the first time in my life anyone ever told me that. I am a good kid. I knew that now.

His Eye is on the Sparrow

After six months at the safe house, Cindy came to get me.

"There are people here to see you. Come to the front room with me."

I could not imagine who would come to visit me. I didn't know that many people.

"Hey, Josh. We've finally come to take you home," Alex said, standing there with Janet. I had a hard time believing my eyes. Were they really standing there to take me with them? Were they serious?

Janet ran to give me a hug.

"We've missed you," she said. They didn't forget me.

I was never so happy to see anyone in my life. I jumped at Alex to hug him.

"We missed you, Josh. We really did miss you," he said in my ear as I hugged him. I never thought I would ever again hear those words.

"The new house is ready and it's even better than before," he said.

"I think you are going to like it," Janet said. "And Corey can't wait to see you."

"Get your things," Alex said. "We have a big surprise at home for all of you."

As we drove to the new house, there was something in the driveway, covered in a large blue tarp. We got out of the car and Alex began to pull the tarp off the massive surprise.

"I thought we would learn a new way to have fun this summer," Alex said as he saw my eyes rest on what was lying beneath the tarp.

A twenty-six foot sailboat was sitting on a trailer just waiting for the ocean to kiss it's hull. I got out of the car and walked around it as it began to sink into my head.

"I got it used," Alex said. "I thought you, Corey and I could fix up a few things it needs and then take it for a spin. Whaddya think?"

I looked at Alex, then back at the boat. I am sure my eyes answered him.

www.ingramcontent.com/pod-product-compliance
Lightning Source LLC
Chambersburg PA
CBHW051235250726
48655CB00006B/2783